Discover China

by Katrina Streza

© 2017 by Katrina Streza
ISBN: 978-1-53240-209-8
eISBN: 978-1-53240-2104
Images licensed from Fotolia.com
All rights reserved.
No portion of this book may be reproduced
without express permission of the publisher.
First Edition
Published in the United States by
Xist Publishing
www.xistpublishing.com
PO Box 61593 Irvine, CA 92602

China is a large country with many people who speak different languages but read using the same script or characters. These characters have changed over time.

4

In the bronze age, Chinese artists began to make pots beautiful. Beauty is important in China.

This screen and this vase were used to make the inside of a house beautiful.

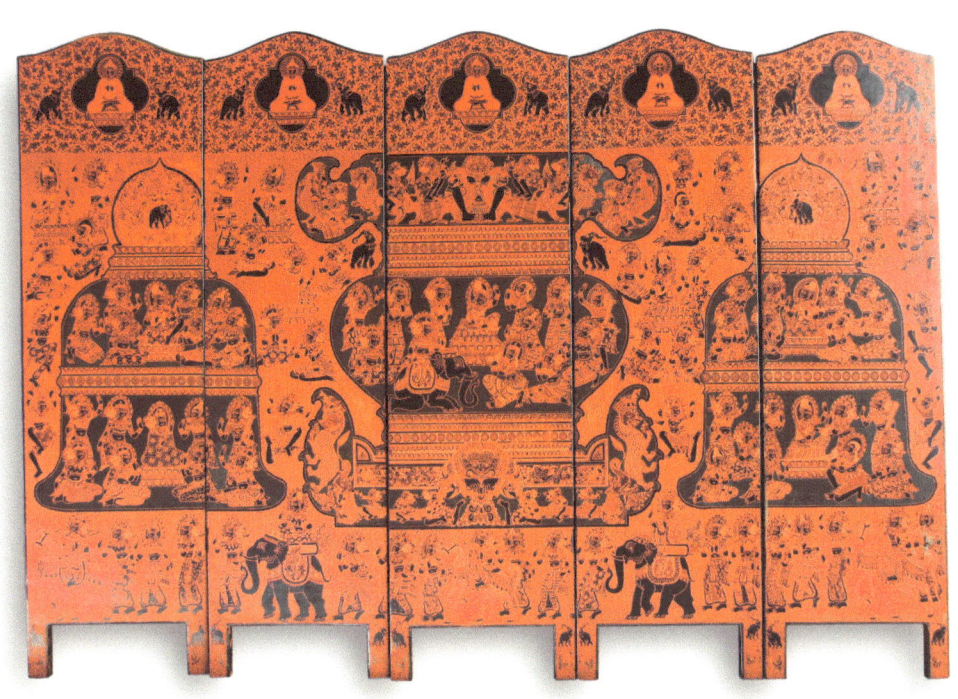

This Pipa was used to make beautiful music. It has four strings.

This Chinese palace has bright colors to show beauty and strength.

11

Chinese gardens try to show that nature is beautiful. This gate into a garden helps people see the beauty.

This bonsai tree is small, but old. Bonsai trees show that beauty can be small.

Lychee fruit are not beautiful, but they are tasty.

The lotus flower is beautiful and reminds people to be pure, like the Buddha.

19

This is a statue of the Buddha. His birthday is a holiday in China.

21

On some Chinese holidays, people use lamps that fly into the sky.

On other Chinese holidays, people use gold coins to make the inside of a house beautiful. Chinese coins once had a hole in the middle.

25

All holidays in China have tea. This tea leaf holder has birds and flowers painted on it.

When people in China sit down to have tea, they always pour for their friends. It is bad luck to pour your own tea.

29

Dragons in China mean good luck and strength. This dragon is made out of gold.

The Great Wall of China shows how strong China has been for many years. It is over 2,000 years old and is over 20,000 km long!

www.ingramcontent.com/pod-product-compliance
Lightning Source LLC
LaVergne TN
LVHW010020070426
835507LV00001B/20